TO:

....

FROM:

....

Inspired by his father's life inspiration

SOWER

The

Follow in His Steps

FRANKLIN GRAHAM

and DONNA LEE TONEY

WORTHY

Introduction

FRANKLIN GRAHAM

JESUS CHRIST IS THE OUTSTANDING PERSONALITY OF ALL TIME," wrote Sholem Asch, Yiddish author and playwright. "In all history, both as Son of God and Son of Man . . . no other teacher—Jewish, Christian, Buddhist, Mohammedan—is still a teacher whose teaching is such a guidepost for the world we live in. Other teachers may have something basic for an Oriental, an Arab, or the Occidental; but every act and word of Jesus has value for all of us. Everything he ever said or did has value for us today and that is something you can say of no other man, dead or alive. There is no easy middle ground to stroll upon. You either accept Jesus or reject him."

While there is no evidence that this famed author was a follower of Jesus Christ, he certainly believed that Jesus was who He claimed to be—and there can be no better setting for the parable of the sower told by Jesus Himself. Scripture says, "Every word of God is flawless" (Proverbs 30:5 NIV).

As Jesus walked the sandy shores of the fishing village with His disciples, it was common for large crowds to gather and follow after Him to hear His words. Some were curious. Some were skeptical. Some were burdened. Some were joyous.

The words of Jesus *challenged* inquiring minds.

His words *convicted* critical spirits.

His words *comforted* weary hearts.

His words *captivated* those who loved Him.

This is the Son of Man sowing the seed of truth into stony hearts and thirsty souls. Perhaps you can picture people gathering. Jesus climbed into a boat and sat looking into faces that had been fashioned by His hands.

His lips longed to speak truth to hearts that were hostile and hearts that were humble.

His eyes peered into souls for which He would soon give His very life to die in their place.

As the waters of Galilee lapped against the boat and the lake breeze brushed across His face, the people standing at the water's edge eagerly listened as the wise Teacher said . . .

"*A sower* went out to sow . . ." (Mark 4:3 ESV).

The parables of Jesus teach us many things and, as with all inspired Scripture, God's Word speaks directly into people's lives in very specific ways.

The lessons that can be gleaned from the parables of Jesus are innumerable. Some say He spoke in riddles, but every word He spoke was truth. His truth overshadowed philosophers. His truth underscored Himself (John 1:1).

Jesus laid aside His glory to walk among men.

His steps carried Him across the plains and hillsides proclaiming forgiveness and salvation for mankind. He sowed good seed in repentant hearts.

His steps carried Him to Calvary, where He laid down His life to save the human race from sin that leads to eternal separation from Almighty God, sowing good seed that establishes a relationship between God and man.

He stepped out of the Garden Tomb on Easter morning, vacating a grave that could not hold the Savior of the world, and sowed the seed of the resurrection that springs forth with new life.

And we are told in Scripture to "follow in his steps" (1 Peter 2:21 ESV).

This is the picture we have in the parable of the sower. Jesus identifies Himself as the Sower of good seed (Matthew 13:37). He set the example of what He desires His followers to do: sow the good seed of the Word of God, the Gospel of Christ.

There have been countless servants who have been obedient to follow Him and to do as He said: "Go into all the world and preach the gospel" (Mark 16:15).

I am grateful that my father, Billy Graham, has been among those who have scattered the good seed of God's Word from city to city, country to country, and continent to continent, following in the steps of Jesus. He often says, "Evangelism is not a calling reserved exclusively for the clergy. I believe the greatest priority of the church today is to mobilize all followers of Christ to do His work. Those who do the work of sowing the seed know that much inevitably falls upon stony ground and bears no fruit, but if only a few seeds flourish, the results are manifold."

Many may not realize that my father sowed seed as a farm boy in Charlotte, North Carolina. There is no question that the Lord implanted his heritage deep into fertile soil.

As a young man he learned the principles of sowing and planting. When God called him to preach the Gospel, he applied what he had learned early in life—preparing, planting, and harvesting. These have served as the blueprint for ministry: prepare the soil in prayer, plant the seed of the Gospel by faith, and harvest souls for God's kingdom.

I trust that this book will be a tool in your hands to help you realize your own potential of sowing seed wherever

your footsteps take you. The story that follows will tap your reserves and put your feet in motion as you step out of your comfort zone and into the fields of harvest, for the time is coming when Christ Himself will step down from the clouds of glory for the great harvest gathering. The task is not confined to preachers and missionaries. We can all be sowers of the seed of the Gospel.

God bless you as you put your hand to the plow and follow in the steps of the Sower.

Franklin Graham

Boone, North Carolina

September 2012

And again {Jesus} began to teach by the sea.
And a great multitude was gathered to Him,
so that He got into a boat and sat in it on the sea;
and the whole multitude was on the land facing the sea.

(MARK 4:1)

IN THE GOSPELS, Jesus is often described as being near the sea. Jesus sat by the sea, walked on the sea, sent unclean spirits into the sea, traveled by sea, and withdrew from great crowds to the sea.

This is where we find Jesus when He told the parable of the sower, the seed, and the soils. Interestingly, He chose the sea as the backdrop to teach about sowing seed. Perhaps it was an unspoken message to the crowd that not even deep waters should prevent us from sowing the seed of the Gospel. Jesus sowed the seed of faith in Peter when the disciples saw Jesus walking on the water during a storm on the sea. They learned from the Miracle Maker that faith conquers fear. When Jesus later told them the parable of the mustard seed (a small seed), He said, "If you have faith as a mustard seed, you can say to this mulberry tree, 'Be pulled up by the roots and be planted in the sea,' and it would obey you" (Luke 17:6). Jesus was sowing faith, not fear. "Therefore with joy you will draw water from the wells of salvation" (Isaiah 12:3).

Scripture teaches that we reap what we sow, and in that sense we are all sowers. While the multitude marveled at Jesus' story, they could not comprehend it. Jesus told His disciples that unless they understood the parable of the sower, they would likely not understand the other parables (Mark 4:13).

The portrait Jesus paints with words in this parable identifies a sower, the seed, and the soils. The Bible says, "Blessed are you who sow beside all waters" (Isaiah 32:20).

What kind of sower are you? Are you sowing the seed of the Good News into the soil . . . or beside the waters?

Jesus
the Teacher

Then {Jesus} taught them many things by parables,

and said to them in His teaching . . .

(MARK 4:2)

AS WE READ GOD'S WORD,

we are inspired by Jesus revealing the heart of His Father in heaven. Jesus was sent to earth to die for the sins of mankind; yet, in the Father's compassion and mercy for man's ignorance of God's love, He also sent His Son to walk among His creation—on land and sea—teaching truths that shed light upon darkened souls. Here at the sea, Jesus looked into sin-sick souls that thirsted for living water and eternal life, but the people could not comprehend the overwhelming love of God. Patiently He taught them. "I will open My mouth in parables; I will utter things kept secret from the foundation of the world" (Matthew 13:35).

Many wonder why Jesus taught using parables. Among the roles Jesus filled while on earth was schoolmaster. He encountered those who did not believe He was the Christ but still called Him "Teacher" (Luke 18:18). And Jesus called even His disciples "children" (John 21:5).

How often do schoolteachers stand before their classes and tell stories as a way to illustrate the lesson? They don't simply ask, "What is ten minus two?" Instead, they draw a picture so that the children can visualize the question. "Johnny picked ten delicious red apples from the tree and then ate two of them. How many are left?" You can just imagine a child holding up ten little fingers and bending two of them down, then carefully counting eight fingers.

Jesus understood the learning style of His listeners, and He spoke to them accordingly. As He walked the countryside, He taught His disciples about what was to come. "Nevertheless I tell you the truth. It is to your advantage that I go away; for if I do not go away, the Helper will not come to you; but if I depart, I will send Him to you. . . . For the Holy Spirit will teach you" (John 16:7; Luke 12:12).

What is the Holy Spirit teaching you through the parables of Jesus in His Word?

Listen! Behold, a sower went out to sow . . .

(MARK 4:3)

JESUS OFTEN IDENTIFIED HIMSELF with farmers. Farming is the first vocation for man the Lord established when He created Adam. He told Adam that he would toil over the land that would produce herbs and thorns—good and bad (Genesis 3:17–18). When Jesus came into the world, He took upon Himself the form of a servant (Philippians 2:7) and sowed good seed in the soil of souls.

In the parable of the wheat and tares (Matthew 13:36–43), Jesus identified Himself as the Sower. His disciples said, "Explain to us the parable" (Matthew 13:36). Jesus answered, "He who sows the good seed is the Son of Man. The field is the world, the good seeds are the sons of the kingdom, but the tares [the bad seeds] are the sons of the wicked one. The enemy who sowed them [the tares] is the devil, the harvest is the end of the age, and the reapers are the angels" (Matthew 13:37–41).

Because of Adam and Eve's sin (disobeying God in the Garden), Satan spoiled the perfection of man's life on earth and he has been sowing seeds of wickedness ever since. Jesus cautioned His followers to beware of those who sow

bad seed (Satan's lies) and warned, "You will know them by their fruits. Do men gather grapes from thornbushes or figs from thistles? Even so, every good tree bears good fruit, but a bad tree bears bad fruit . . . every tree that does not bear good fruit is cut down and thrown into the fire. Therefore by their fruits you will know them" (Matthew 7:16–20).

We must pray for the Lord's discernment in our relationships and in our step-by-step walk with God. It is only through His enlightenment that we can recognize the fruit that reveals His nature.

Is the good seed of the Gospel being sown into and nourished in your heart?

Jesus
the Source

And it happened, as he sowed, that some seed
fell by the wayside; and the birds of the air
came and devoured it.

(MARK 4:4)

WHEN BUILDING THEIR NESTS, birds fly on a scavenger hunt for twigs, clods of mud, and wet, leafy compresses. They swoop into tree branches to set up house for a season and scout the landscape to find seeds for themselves and worms for their young. Jesus uses birds throughout Scripture to teach lessons and give illustrations about His truth; for the Lord feeds the fowl of the air and tells us that we are more valuable to Him than the birds He watches over (Matthew 6:26).

Preparation of the soil is important to one who invests in seed with the hope of producing a bountiful harvest. A sower is careful about the art of sowing and planting in good soil, but a sower cannot control the wind that sweeps away scattered seed. A sower cannot stop rain from gushing through a freshly plowed field, dislodging a day's labor. Nor can a farmer shoo birds from eating his freshly planted crop.

There are many principles and methods for sowing seed. Some seeds need to be buried in the ground; other seed can be scattered and still take root. Yet ravens, crows, and vultures have a keen radar and prey upon a farmer's toil, pilfering seed wherever it lands. While God can use a raven as an agent of good, as in the case of the ravens feeding Elijah (1 Kings 17:4), Satan can use such a bird as an agent of evil. In this case, we see the birds of the air snatching away the seed of the Gospel.

This is the picture Jesus gives us in the parable. The sower went out to sow . . . but some seed fell by the wayside, ground that had been trampled by foot and was too hardened for the seed to grow (Luke 8:5), so the birds snatched up the seed. The seed that feeds the birds will never take root to produce a bountiful harvest.

When the seed of the Gospel falls upon the soil of your soul, do you let it feed the birds or are you nourishing it with the things of God?

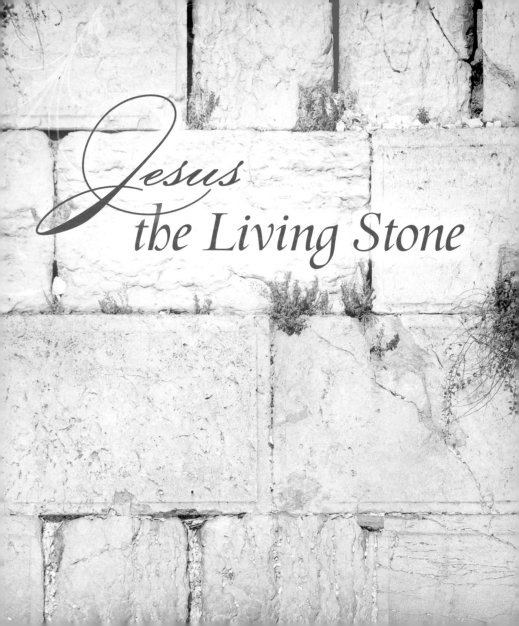

Some {seed} fell on stony ground,
where it did not have much earth;
and immediately it sprang up because it
had no depth of earth.

(MARK 4:5)

THE BIBLE MAKES MANY REFERENCES TO STONES. There were stone tablets for lawgiving and stone altars for worship, engraved stones for memorializing and smooth stones for slaying a giant. There were stone foundations for kings' palaces and a stone that sealed the tomb of the King of kings . . . but only for a brief time. There were stones that caused the foot to stumble and the Cornerstone that secured our foundation. There were millstones of violence and stones surrounding the throne of the Prince of Peace. There were stones of death and the living stones mentioned in 1 Peter 2:5.

But here in the parable of the sower, Jesus describes seed that falls on ground that has been strewn with stones. Stones absorb water, so when seed falls into stony ground, it is robbed of moisture and has little soil to take root. This is what happens to the Seed of Truth—the Word of God—when it falls on hard and stony hearts. The Bible says that we are to feed upon the Word of God (Job 23:12). While

we are sowing the Gospel where our feet carry us, we should pray that the seed will fall on fertile ground—ground that has been plowed by prayer for the lost. Jesus said that if we are silent in our witness of Him, the very stones will cry out and proclaim His salvation (Luke 19:40).

Are you praying that the power of God would both soften the soil of your heart and water your prayers with tears of compassion for dry and hardened hearts that need to be tenderized?

But when the sun was up {the seed} was scorched,

and because it had no root it withered away.

(MARK 4:6)

THE LORD SEES WHAT WE DO WITH what He has given. In the parable of the talents (Matthew 25:14–30), Jesus described how a master gave three servants different values of talents (a form of money) and trusted they would use them wisely. The first two increased what they had been given. The last servant did nothing with what he was given. When the master returned, the last servant excused his laziness by claiming he had protected it out of fear of the master. The master rebuked the lazy servant for his untruthful representation, claiming that he reaped where he had not sown and had gathered where he had not scattered seed.

Here is the picture of seed that had nothing from which to draw, burned up by the heat of the day. Imagine opening a bag of fresh sunflower seeds and scattering them on parched ground. Unless they are confiscated by wildlife, the seeds will dry up and be blown away by the wind.

Many listening to the story had no understanding. They could not grasp the lessons Jesus was teaching about the sower, seed, and soils. Sometimes we don't even realize where we are sowing the seed of the Gospel. Perhaps we've talked to a family member, neighbor, or fellow worker about what God has done in our lives, but they do not take it to heart. The good seed we sow lands on dry ground. Time passes and we forget about their dehydrated souls. The world's system has drained their hearts of spiritual nutrients. Or perhaps they offend us and we retaliate in a harsh way. We use careless words to satisfy our position. Our testimony is scorched

by human anger instead of demonstrating God's spirit of forgiveness. We are to exemplify Christ living in us every moment of every day. You may say, "That is impossible!" But it isn't impossible if we remember *who* we belong to. It is not impossible if we live each moment with the knowledge that He is closer to us than any family member, neighbor, or acquaintance; for the Holy Spirit of the Living God, whom we say we serve, resides within our hearts.

How are you scattering the seed of the Gospel through your testimony?

And some seed fell among thorns;
and the thorns grew up and choked it,
and it yielded no crop.

(MARK 4:7)

IF YOU'VE EVER STEPPED INTO A BRIER PATCH, you understand what thorns do to human flesh. When you're fortunate to get untangled, the pinheads of the thorns seem to run with you. The only time in Scripture that a thorn was used for good comes from the apostle Paul: "Lest I should be exalted . . . a thorn in the flesh was given to me, a messenger of Satan to buffet me. . . . [The Lord] said to me, 'My grace is sufficient for you.' . . . Therefore most gladly I will rather boast in my infirmities, that the power of Christ may rest upon me" (2 Corinthians 12:7–9).

We know that Paul did not have a literal thorn piercing his skin, but whatever his infirmity, it stung as though a thorn ripping the flesh. Paul identifies the "thorn" as a "messenger of Satan." No wonder the Bible speaks of thorns and snares, a wilderness of thorns, a fire of thorns, a hedge of thorns, and sadly—a crown of thorns. Jeremiah prophesied the words of the Lord: "Break up your fallow ground, and do not sow among thorns" (Jeremiah 4:3). The prophet challenged the hardened hearts of God's people to break up the thorn-sown ground and make it useful for sowing good seed.

We *reflect* on the darkness at Calvary when the Lord Jesus hung on the cross with a twisted "crown of thorns . . . on His head. . . . And they bowed the knee before Him and mocked Him, saying, 'Hail, King of the Jews!'" (Matthew 27:29). Jesus bore the thorns of our sin. But we also *rejoice* for the harvest is coming. There is healing from the piercing of the thorns. "Behold . . . on the cloud sat One like the Son of Man, having on His head a golden crown, and in His hand a sharp sickle. And another angel . . . crying with a loud voice to Him. . . . 'Thrust in Your sickle and reap . . . for the harvest of the earth is ripe'" (Revelation 14:14–15). You see, there is hope. "At the name of Jesus every knee should bow . . . and . . . every tongue should confess that Jesus Christ is Lord" (Philippians 2:10–11).

When the seed of the Gospel falls upon thorn-filled hearts, the truth is pricked against the thorn-seeded lies of Satan and a battle is waged for the soul. Satan will do all within his power to keep the seed from taking root, often victorious in winning a soul for his realm of everlasting darkness. Christians, through the power of Christ, must warn others of the brier patches that entrap the lost. The Lord said to Ezekiel, "And you, son of man, do not be afraid of them nor be afraid of their words, though briers and thorns are with you. . . . You shall speak My words to them, whether they hear or whether they refuse" (Ezekiel 2:6–7).

What will you do to spread the seed of the Gospel in the thorn-filled ground where others are walking?

But other seed fell on good ground and yielded a crop that sprang up, increased and produced: some thirtyfold, some sixty, and some a hundred.

(MARK 4:8)

THE NUMBER OF SOULS REACHED FOR THE KINGDOM of God is incalculable. As the parable of the talents proclaims, the master does not hold his stewards responsible for the results, but He does reward them for their faithfulness (Matthew 25:23). We sow, we plant, and we water the seed of the Gospel with our prayers for the lost and our songs of praise for the saved.

All glory for the winning of souls belongs to the Savior of our souls, the Lord Jesus Christ; for even the seed—the Word of God—is given to the sower to spread around the world, scatter along the pathway, and plant deep into the hearts of mankind. The book of Isaiah says, "For as the rain comes down, and the snow from heaven . . . [to] water the earth, and make it bring forth and bud, that it may give seed to the sower . . . so shall My word be that goes forth from My mouth; it shall not return to Me void, but it shall accomplish what I please, and it shall prosper in the thing for which I sent it" (Isaiah 55:10–11).

Jesus set the example of what a sower of the seed is to be. He sowed seed with each step He took. He said, "I am the light of the world. He who follows Me shall not walk in darkness, but have the light of life" (John 8:12). The footsteps of Jesus are sure and because this is true, we can walk by faith with assurance that He is with us. "As you therefore have received Christ Jesus the Lord, so walk in Him, rooted and built up in Him and established in the faith" (Colossians

2:6–7). With great joy we can follow His example in sowing seeds of faith that lead others to the One who has sown His love into the fields where *truth* is planted.

The Bible says, "Those who sow in tears shall reap in joy. He who continually goes forth weeping, bearing seed for sowing, shall doubtless come again with rejoicing, bringing his sheaves with him" (Psalm 126:5–6).

Will you put Jesus Christ ahead of each step you take as you sow the seed of His Gospel through His fields of harvest?

Jesus
the Preacher

And {Jesus} said to them,

"He who has ears to hear, let him hear!"

(MARK 4:9)

WHEN THE LORD JESUS CHRIST TAUGHT in the synagogue, He read the Scriptures aloud, quoting from Isaiah: "The Spirit of the LORD is upon Me, because He has anointed Me to preach the gospel to the poor; He has sent Me to heal the brokenhearted, to proclaim liberty to the captives and recovery of sight to the blind, to set at liberty those who are oppressed. . . . Today this Scripture is fulfilled in your hearing. So all bore witness to Him, and marveled at the gracious words which proceeded out of His mouth" (Luke 4:18, 21–22).

Jesus was sowing the seed of the Gospel in the *most likely* location—a place of worship. He planted in the hearts of the hearers His reason for coming to earth in the form of man—so they could hear the Word of God. He sowed the Gospel seed in many ways: with rich mercy in the hearts of the poor; with healing into broken hearts; with freedom to those in captivity; with light into the eyes of the blind; and with comfort to those oppressed. The hearers rejoiced at Jesus' words filled with hope and consolation—until He spoke of this same grace being extended to the Gentiles. Those present suddenly did not want to hear the rest of the story. They were indignant. The Bible says they were "filled with wrath" (Luke 4:28).

This is what Jesus was saying in the parable of the sower. Many did not want to hear the truth, so they tuned out the words of Jesus; they hardened the soil of their souls to His message. The Bible tells us that if we will open our hearts to God's Word, He will give understanding to the deaf and sight to the blind (Matthew 11:4–5).

Is the soil of your soul prepared to receive what Christ desires to give?

Jesus
the Discerner
of Hearts

But when ⸓Jesus⸓ was alone,

those around Him with the twelve asked

Him about the parable.

(MARK 4:10)

JESUS KNEW THE HARDENED HEARTS OF THOSE WHO TURNED AWAY. Many came hoping to see miracles. They wanted to be *wowed* by watching a lame man walk; they wanted to watch the thrill of a blind man opening his eyes to faces he had never seen. There is nothing wrong with wanting to see the miracle-working Teacher in action, but the crowd around Jesus wanted only the breathtaking amazement of witnessing Jesus at work. They were not interested in learning the lessons He was sowing along the sun-drenched paths He trod. The Bible says, "The natural man does not receive the things of the Spirit of God, for they are foolishness to him; nor can he know them, because they are spiritually discerned" (1 Corinthians 2:14). "They will turn their ears away from the truth" (2 Timothy 4:4).

But when Jesus was alone with those who sincerely desired the truth, He patiently explained the meaning of the parable. The Lord knows the intention of our hearts and it's important that we seek understanding of His Word. The parables teach about the one sowing the Word of God, the one hearing the Word of God, and the One who is the Word of God. "In the beginning was the Word, and the Word was with God, and the Word was God" (John 1:1).

Most parents are overjoyed when a child comes asking for help with his homework. Parents want their children to learn; they cannot successfully comprehend many things without instruction, nor can adults understand all things. The Lord must have been pleased when those close to Him asked for further explanation. The psalmist said, "Teach me Your way, O LORD; I will walk in Your truth" (Psalm 86:11). The Lord promised that He would send the Spirit to teach us (John 14:26).

Are you listening to what the Sower of the seed is teaching?

Jesus the Sower of Understanding

And {Jesus} said to them, "To you it has been given to know the mystery of the kingdom of God; but to those who are outside, all things come in parables."

(MARK 4:11)

PEOPLE TEND TO HEAR only what they want to hear. Jesus recognized this dimension of human nature, realizing that few desired to know the deeper meaning of what He said. It wasn't the parables but the nuggets of truth in them that they turned their ears from. Jesus said, "Unless a grain of wheat falls into the ground and dies, it remains alone; but if it dies, it produces much grain" (John 12:24). To farmers this principle was clear, but to those who had never turned a spade of soil, the lesson could be missed. Paul picked up on this when he said, "What you sow is not made alive unless it dies" (1 Corinthians 15:36), teaching the principle that when seed is planted in the ground it dies and regenerates, bringing new life.

Jesus said, "A little while longer the light is with you. . . . I still have many things to say to you, but you cannot bear them now . . . a little while, and you will not see Me; and again a little while, and you will see Me, because I go to the Father" (John 12:35; 16:12, 16). The disciples did not understand until He said, "I say to you that you will weep and lament, but the world will rejoice; and you will be sorrowful, but your sorrow will be turned into joy. . . . The time is coming when I will no longer speak to you in figurative language, but I will tell you plainly about the Father. . . . I came forth from the Father and have come into the world. Again, I leave the world and go to the Father" (John 16:20, 25, 28).

Jesus identified Himself as the Light of the World but predicted that the world would rejoice at His death, not realizing that the grave would hold Him only to His appointed time—three days. He told the disciples that they would abandon Him out of fear—leaving Him alone. Then He foretold of His coming resurrection to life anew. This truth would give final and eternal explanation to the principle of the grain of wheat that dies in order to produce much grain (fruit). For in Jesus' death and resurrection, the truth He had implanted in others brought forth seed that was scattered abroad, producing laborers for the fields and fruit for the kingdom.

Likewise, "The body is *sown* in corruption, it is raised in incorruption. It is *sown* in dishonor, it is raised in glory. It is *sown* in weakness, it is raised in power. It is *sown* a natural body, it is raised a spiritual body" (1 Corinthians 15:42–44).

Are you sowing Gospel seed to bear fruit for God's kingdom?

Jesus
the Rejected One

. . . so that "seeing they may see and not perceive,
and hearing they may hear and not understand;
lest they should turn, and their sins be forgiven them."

(MARK 4:12)

JESUS OFFERS ALL PEOPLE THE GIFT OF HIS FORGIVING LOVE. What makes mankind reject God's salvation? Many answers could be offered, but they would *all* boil down to this: men love darkness rather than light because their deeds are evil (John 3:19). The Bible says, "For *all* have sinned and fall short of the glory of God" (Romans 3:23). In order for people to accept God they must first admit that they are sinners condemned before the righteous Judge. It is hard for many to reconcile that the righteous Judge is also the God of love. Human nature tends to gravitate toward excuses—*If God loves me He will make me good . . . If He loves me He certainly won't condemn me.*

This is what Jesus was saying to His listeners. Those who rejected His truth were more than satisfied to take the food He offered when He fed the five thousand, but they did not want to feed on His Word. They wanted to be recipients of His miracle-working power, but they did not want to suffer for His name's sake. They wanted to enjoy the riches of eternal life, but they did not want to lay down their sinful lives in exchange for sacrificial and holy lives.

Jesus used parables to draw the true believers out of the

crowd. Those who didn't care to understand simply turned away. Those who sought for truth begged, "Tell us more!" Some saw the miracles but chose to ignore their purpose. They saw, but did not perceive. They heard, but did not understand. If they would only choose to identify with Him and turn from their sins, they would be forgiven, but their willing sinfulness bound them to the world's empty lie. These represent the soil of unrepentant hearts in which the seed of the Gospel cannot take root.

Are you praying for Jesus to cultivate the soil of unrepentant hearts so that the seed of the Gospel will take root and flourish?

And {Jesus} said to them,
"Do you not understand this parable?
How then will you understand all the parables?"

(MARK 4:13)

JESUS TAUGHT INFALLIBLE TRUTH IN PARABLE FORM. His parables were not concocted stories; they were lessons meticulously wrapped in the law of God and tied together with heavenly hope. "Give ear, O my people, to my law; incline your ears to the words of my mouth. I will open my mouth in a parable; I will utter dark sayings of old . . . make them known . . . that the generation to come might know them . . . that they may set their hope in God and not forget the works of God" (Psalm 78:1–2, 5–7). This was written centuries before the Lord Jesus walked upon the earth in human form, and here we see a prophecy fulfilled in the parable of the sower and "all the parables."

Among the evidence that the Bible is infallible is the fact that the inspired writers did not cover up the truth of even their own sin, referred to as "dark sayings of old." At one time or another we all tell on ourselves. This is clearly revealed in the pages of Scripture. Many think of a storyteller as one who exaggerates the facts. Jesus—

the sinless One—holds His listeners spellbound by *His story* . . . for He knows human nature like no other, and biblical *history* gives account to the sinless One, redeeming the sinful . . . one by one.

Someone defined a parable this way: "an earthly story with a heavenly meaning." Parables have greater impact when seen in light of man's iniquity and God's infallibility. We see this in the parable of the lost son, which is a clear picture of the Lord welcoming a repentant child *home*. This young man sowed wild seed—he lost his joy of living—but then he returned to his father.

Do you know some who are sowing the wrong seed in the wrong field? Are you praying for them to return home to the Sower?

The sower sows the word.

(MARK 4:14)

JESUS DESCRIBES THE SEED as "the word of God" (Luke 8:11). As Jesus trekked throughout the land and saw great numbers following Him, He opened His mouth with parables—and plowed the soil of human hearts, planting seed—the very words of God.

If you were to circle common phrases in many of Jesus' parables you would make this discovery: there are *kingdom* threads woven through the parables. They aren't clever thoughts; they are clear truths. The Lord was not entertaining the throngs. He was sowing *kingdom* seed.

"The kingdom of heaven *is like a man* who sowed good seed . . ." (Matthew 13:24); "The kingdom of heaven *is like a mustard seed*, which a man took and sowed in his field . . ." (Matthew 13:31); "The kingdom of heaven *is like* leaven, which *a woman* took and hid . . ." (Matthew 13:33); "The kingdom of heaven *is like treasure* hidden in a field . . ." (Matthew 13:44); "The kingdom of heaven *is like a merchant* seeking beautiful pearls . . . " (Matthew 13:45); "The kingdom of heaven *is like a dragnet* that was cast into the sea . . ." (Matthew 13:47); "The kingdom of heaven *is like a certain king* who wanted to settle accounts with his servants . . ." (Matthew 18:23); "The kingdom of heaven *is like a landowner* who went out early in the morning to hire laborers for his vineyard . . ." (Matthew 20:1); "The kingdom of heaven *is like* a *certain king* who arranged a marriage for his son, and sent out his servants to call those who were invited to the wedding . . ." (Matthew 22:2–3);

"The kingdom of heaven *shall be likened to ten virgins* who . . . went out to meet the bridegroom . . ." (Matthew 25:1); "For the kingdom of heaven *is like a man* traveling to a far country, who called his own servants and delivered his goods to them" (Matthew 25:14).

These are not fairy tales. Jesus gives us glimpses of His kingdom. Jesus speaks of individuals: merchants, landowners, laborers, and kings. Jesus tells of far countries and vineyards. He tells of hidden treasures, settling accounts, and delivering goods. He tells of weddings . . . and the bridegroom. Simply put, He is sowing the seed of the Gospel of His kingdom in the hearts of the hearers.

How has the Sower planted the seed of the Gospel in your heart through these parables?

Jesus
Identifies the Thief

And these are the ones by the wayside where the word is sown.

When they hear, Satan comes immediately and takes away

the word that was sown in their hearts.

(MARK 4:15)

LUKE RECORDS THE SAME ACCOUNT
this way: "Those by the wayside are the ones who hear; then the devil comes and takes away the word out of their hearts, lest they should believe and be saved" (8:12). This is *stolen seed.*

Satan will do everything in his power to turn a soul away from the Lord "according to the working of Satan, with all power, signs, and lying wonders, and with all unrighteous deception among those who perish, because they did not receive the love of the truth, that they might be saved" (2 Thessalonians 2:9–10).

This is the business that Satan is in and he's good at it. But take careful note that while Satan is powerful, he is not *all-powerful*; that realm belongs only to God (Job 2:6). The Bible says that God will destroy Satan, who has the power of death, releasing those subject to bondage (Hebrews 2:14).

Jesus sent the apostle Paul to the people of the world to sow "the love of the truth" because they were in bondage to Satan's lies. The Lord was blessing His word through Paul's ministry "to turn them from darkness to light, and from the power of Satan to God, that they may receive forgiveness of sins . . . by faith in Me" (Acts 26:18). But as convincing as Paul was, some mocked him and turned away (Acts 17:32). This illustrates seed of the Word of God that is stolen by Satan.

Are you praying for those who are in Satan's clutches, that the seed will penetrate and take root in their hearts?

Jesus
Proclaims

These likewise are the ones sown on stony ground who,
when they hear the word,
immediately receive it with gladness.

(MARK 4:16)

IMAGINE PAUL STANDING BEFORE KING AGRIPPA, the son of King Herod who had the apostle James beheaded. Paul had been arrested for preaching Christ and was brought before Agrippa to defend himself. The King said, "You are permitted to speak" (Acts 26:1). What an opportunity! How did Paul respond? He sowed the seed of the Gospel in the heart of the king. He lived out Psalm 119:46: "I will speak of Your testimonies also before kings." Paul boldly asked, "King Agrippa, do you believe the prophets?" Paul knew that if Agrippa said yes, the king would give indication that he believed in the One the prophets predicted would come—the One whom Paul proclaimed. Then Agrippa said to Paul, "You almost persuade me to become a Christian" (Acts 26:27–28).

Agrippa was captivated by the Word of God. He even thought Paul innocent of the charges against him. The seed of truth had fallen into the soil of the king's heart, but he didn't take hold of it—the seed did not take root. He "did not believe in God, and did not trust in His salvation" (Psalm 78:22). This is the picture of *wasted seed*. "So are the paths of all who forget God. . . . His roots wrap around the rock heap, and look for a place in the stones" (Job 8:13, 17).

Whether we speak before royalty or relatives, friends or foes, the Bible says, "Come and hear, all you who fear God, and I will declare what He has done for my soul" (Psalm 66:16). This testimony of the power of God in our lives is a faith-packed seed that has the potential of taking root in another's heart. Whether it does or doesn't, exercise the right to speak, as Paul did.

Will you pray, as Paul did in Acts 26:29, that all who hear the truth might become Christians?

Jesus
Knows

*. . . they have no root in themselves,
and so endure only for a time. Afterward,
when tribulation or persecution arises for the word's sake,
immediately they stumble.*

(MARK 4:17)

THE WORD *IMMEDIATELY* IS USED FOUR TIMES in the parable of the sower. *Immediately*, without thought or reflection, they receive the Word of God, but the first time trials come because of their association with God's Word, they falter. Their faith in God is on shallow ground and they stumble over rocks of disbelief. They presented themselves on the outside as Christians but there was no connection to the power of God's Word to help them overcome. Instead of relying on what they claimed to believe, they turned away—the seed did not take root. Just as the Old Testament records Israel's rejection of good, the Bible says, "The enemy will pursue him. . . . They sow the wind, and reap the whirlwind" (Hosea 8:3, 7).

As Jesus sowed His Word into the hearts of His listeners, He knew where the seed was taking root and where seed was blowing in the wind. "He who eats this bread [the Word of God] will live forever. . . . Does this offend you?" Jesus asked (John 6:58, 61). "The words that I speak to you are spirit, and they are life. But there are some of you who do not believe" (John 6:63–64). Some resented that He knew the intent of their hearts and their lack of belief—and from that time, many of His followers "walked with Him no more" (John 6:66).

Others who claim salvation in Christ walk with the Lord while life is good. But when life doesn't meet their expectations—whether it's bad health, a lost job, or a wayward child—they abandon the faith and "[walk] with Him no more." This is what Jesus was saying in the parable: "When tribulation or persecution arises because of the word, *immediately* he stumbles" (Matthew 13:21). The seed had landed on stony ground.

Will you pray and ask the Lord to direct the Gospel seed you are casting along your paths?

Jesus
Observes
the Hearers

Now these are the ones sown among thorns;
they are the ones who hear the word . . .

(MARK 4:18)

JESUS DESCRIBED SEED THAT FALLS
into the hearts of four types of people: the first, "the ones
who hear" (Luke 8:12); the second, "when they hear" (Luke
8:13); the third, "when they have heard" (Luke 8:14); and
the last, "having heard the word" (Luke 8:15). This is a
wonderful picture of the Word of God being "heard." The
not-so-wonderful picture is what three types of people do
with what they have heard. The first group hears the truth
but doesn't embrace it, welcoming in the thief. The second
group hears the truth and welcomes it, but when the thrill
wears off they wander away. The third group hears but
welcomes worldly distractions that crowd their minds and

feed their desires. The fourth group hears the word and feeds on it, causing the good seed to bear good fruit.

This third group has something in common with the children of Israel. They were thriving, sowing seeds of pleasure for themselves and bearing no fruit. The Bible says, "They have sown wheat but reaped thorns . . . be ashamed of your harvest" (Jeremiah 12:13). "Tremble, you . . . who are at ease . . . beat your breasts for the pleasant fields . . . for the soil of my people growing up in thorns and briers" (Isaiah 32:11–13 ESV).

Many churchgoers today are in this category. They have heard the Word of God; yet they mix the Word with error, feeding on worldly pleasures that choke the truth and drain the life out of the seed. This group often goes unnoticed by God's people, who assume they are obedient followers of Christ.

The truth is that Satan plants bad seed inside the church, introducing distractions that trample and bruise the good seed of God's Word. Satan cannot pluck the root of good seed from God's fields of harvest, but he can and does sow tares (pretenders) in our churches, many times rendering God's people ineffective because they too become distracted by things other than the Word of the living God. They "have run greedily in . . . error . . . while they feast with you without fear, serving only themselves. They are . . . late autumn trees without fruit, twice dead, pulled up by the roots; raging waves of the sea, foaming up their own shame" (Jude 11–13).

Will you pray for wisdom to distinguish Satan's bad seed and rotten fruit from the fruit of the Spirit that blossoms from the good seed of God's Word?

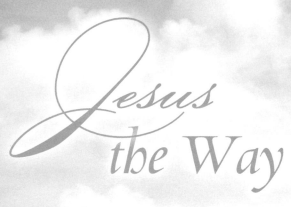

Jesus
the Way

. . . and the cares of this world, the deceitfulness of riches,
and the desires for other things entering in choke the word,
and it becomes unfruitful.

(MARK 4:19)

THIS VERSE MIRRORS THE REALITY of the rich young ruler who asked Jesus, "Good Teacher, what shall I do that I may inherit eternal life?" (Mark 10:17). This young man obviously had heard God's Word and thought he was a prime candidate for the gift Jesus offered—eternal life. He thought he was good enough to enter into God's promise of forgiveness, without repenting. This is *selfish seed*. But when Jesus looked at him *with love* and told him that he lacked one thing: "Go *your way*, sell whatever you have . . . take up the cross, and follow Me" (Mark 10:21), the young man's feet were planted firmly in the soil of his *own way*. He wasn't willing to exchange his way for God's way. Jesus said, "I am the way" (John 14:6). The deceitfulness of riches had choked the Word of God, which says, "Here is the man who did not make God his strength, but trusted in the abundance of his riches" (Psalm 52:7). It wasn't the young man's wealth that was wrong; it was his loyalty to his riches that was wrong. He couldn't serve two masters. "No one can serve two masters; for either he will hate the one and love the other, or else he will be loyal to the one and despise the other. You cannot serve God and mammon" (Matthew 6:24). He wasn't willing to lay aside *his way* for *the way*.

Life is richer when seeds of selflessness are sown. Doing good unto others, as the Bible commands, reaps a bountiful harvest. This is what the young man would have learned if he had chosen to follow Jesus instead of being enslaved by his riches. He would have learned that the seed Jesus was about to sow at Calvary would sprout in his heart. The path to Calvary was going to seed the fertile soil of searching souls and bring forth the fruit of eternal life. "Do not be deceived, God is not mocked; for whatever a man sows, that he will also reap. For he who sows to his flesh will of the flesh reap corruption, but he who sows to the Spirit will of the Spirit reap everlasting life" (Galatians 6:7–8).

Are you ready to sow the seed of God's truth in others when they ask, "What must I do to inherit everlasting life?"

But these are the ones sown on good ground,
those who hear the word, accept it, and bear fruit:
some thirtyfold, some sixty, and some a hundred.

(MARK 4:20)

WE CAN PICTURE JESUS AT THIS MOMENT, perhaps with a smile on His face as He spoke of the seed yielding abundant fruit. He had delivered some soul-searching thoughts to those hearing this parable, and it must have pleased the Lord to speak of the good fruit that comes from the good seed—souls harvested from preaching the Gospel. *This is yielded seed*—hearts emptied of all distractions of the world and dedicated to the things of Christ. Hearts emptied of self-pleasure and spilling over with a desire to pursue the lost. Hearts drained of the cares of life and filled with continual praise to the Lord.

Perhaps when Jesus concluded this parable He was picturing heaven filled with the fruits of the vine. After all, He had told His followers, "I am the vine, you are the branches. He who abides in Me, and I in him, bears much fruit" (John 15:5). He also told them, "I go to prepare a place for you" (John 14:2). No one can fathom the harvest of plenty to come.

The Lord has given us in His Word all that we need for this life. But Scripture tells us that "there are also many other things that Jesus did, which if they were written one by one . . . even the world itself could not contain the books that would be written" (John 21:25). This truth should compel us to be effective sowers and bountiful fruit bearers.

Is your heart plowed, prepared, and planted with the good seed of God's Word?

Jesus
Is Love

The fruit of the Spirit is love.

(GALATIANS 5:22)

WHEN THE SOWER'S SEED TAKES ROOT IN OUR SOULS, it flourishes and produces a bountiful harvest of the fruit of the Spirit. The Bible describes this fruit in Galatians 5. We have been injected with the Spirit of love. When the Spirit of God takes up residence in our hearts, He sows the seeds of His attributes into the fertile soil of our thoughts, our speech, our attitudes and actions. This is the result of His transforming power and we must not resist the pruning He does to bring the fruit of His Spirit into every area of our lives. Scripture embodies the seed and fruit, planting and harvesting, weeding out wild briers and gathering in sweetened kernels. Whether we realize it or not, these are things we are and things we do. We all sow seed through our actions—bad or good. We all bring forth fruit through our attitudes—rotten or sweet. We all plant words, in the minds of others, with a hateful spirit or a loving heart. We all harvest thorns or blossoms that affect our thinking. We should all weed out the unlovely within and gather up the sweetness of Him.

The fruit of the Spirit of the living God is love. When Christ comes into our forgiven hearts, sin is removed and the sweet sap of God's love fills the reservoir of our hearts. When a farmer harvests sap from a maple tree, he chisels a hole through the bark and into the tree trunk. He plunges into it a curved piece of wood or rubber, then attaches a bucket or rubber hose and allows the sap to run free into a catch basin. If the farmer is tapping multiple trees, large vats are standing ready to receive the sweet taste of the harvest. This is a picture of what Christ does in the lives of those who receive His seed of love. Through the greatest act of love ever demonstrated, Jesus hung—from splintered wood of His own creation—by nails thrust through His flesh. He was pierced by our sin and, in response, His precious blood was spilled out, covering the sins of all who are ready to receive the sweetness of this greatest attribute—*love*.

Do we exhibit sacrificial love that puts things and others before our own desires? Sowing this kind of love will turn the spade of dirt, exposing the seed of the Gospel to the nutrients of God's great love. But until we ourselves are sown with the love of God, the seed we sow will be wasted. The Lord says, "Indeed I am for you . . . and you shall be tilled and sown. I will multiply men upon you" (Ezekiel 36:9–10).

Do you fully trust God's love to till the soil of your soul?

The fruit of the Spirit is . . . joy.

(GALATIANS 5:22)

WHEN THE SOWER IMPLANTS HIS SEED IN OUR HEARTS, we become infused with the Spirit of joy. Many today interchange the words *joy* and *happiness*, but joy is something that has the ability to fill us even in the midst of unhappy circumstances. Joy is a condition of contentment. Jesus exemplified this in a way that challenges the human spirit. "Jesus . . . for the joy that was set before Him endured the cross" (Hebrews 12:2).

Joy was the fruit of Christ's willingness to sacrificially bear our agony. He did it *joyfully* because He knew the end result—His death was going to bear everlasting fruit—the redeemed. "Behold, this is the joy of His way, and out of the earth others will grow" (Job 8:19).

True joy can only be found in the Lord Jesus Christ. He is the source of joy—"that they may have My joy fulfilled in themselves" (John 17:13). Joy comes from His Word. "Your word was to me . . . joy" (Jeremiah 15:16). Joy is empowered by God's Spirit. "Now may the God of hope fill you with all joy and peace in believing . . . by the power of the Holy Spirit" (Romans 15:13).

The Bible assures us that when the seed of the Gospel takes root in the fertile soil of our heart, it will flourish with the fruit of joy—in times of trials, "You became followers . . . of the Lord, having received the word in much affliction, with joy of the Holy Spirit" (1 Thessalonians 1:6); in the midst of our work, "We . . . are fellow workers for your joy" (2 Corinthians 1:24); and as we grow older, "It is good and fitting . . . to enjoy the good of all his labor . . . all the days of his life which God gives him; for it is his heritage . . . this is the gift of God . . . God keeps him busy with the joy of his heart" (Ecclesiastes 5:18–20).

The Bible speaks of the joy of faith (Philippians 1:25); the voice of joy (Jeremiah 33:11); the sound of joy (Psalm 89:15); and the joy of harvest (Isaiah 9:3). The Bible tells us that we can ask for our joy to be full (John 16:24), and promises that no one will take joy from us (John 16:22).

Are you sowing the Gospel seed in your sphere of influence with joy, anticipating a bountiful harvest?

Jesus Is Peace

The fruit of the Spirit is . . . peace.

(GALATIANS 5:22)

AS THE SOWER'S SEED GROWS

and expands in our souls, we are ingrained with the Spirit of peace. No one person meets the expectation of the Standard-Bearer, the Lord Jesus Christ. The world wants peace, so it claims; yet wars rage—proving that men are incapable of governing themselves. This is the reason Jesus came, to save men from themselves.

His very name speaks of this fruit of the Spirit—He is the God of peace (Romans 15:33); King of peace (Hebrews 7:2); Prince of Peace (Isaiah 9:6). Who better to teach us the fruit of peace? He is our peace (Ephesians 2:14), and He has called us to peace (1 Corinthians 7:15). Why then are we so often at odds with people, circumstances, society, and even ourselves? Perhaps it is because we don't embrace the Peacemaker—to believe and follow His example.

We are told in Scripture to seek peace (Psalm 34:14); to love peace (Zechariah 8:19); to speak peace (Zechariah 9:10); to pursue peace (Hebrews 12:14); to be at peace (1 Thessalonians 5:13); and to go in peace (Mark 5:34).

The Bible tells us that peace is God's blessing (Psalm 29:11). He promised to give us peace in believing (Romans 15:13); peace of thought (Jeremiah 29:11); peace in sleep

(Psalm 4:8); an abundance of peace (Psalm 37:11); peace within our walls (Psalm 122:7); peace within our borders (Psalm 147:14); and peace in heaven (Luke 19:38).

Jesus proclaimed, "Blessed are the peacemakers" (Matthew 5:9); "Have peace with one another" (Mark 9:50); "Peace, be still" (Mark 4:39); and often He greeted people with the phrase, "Peace to you" (Luke 24:36).

Is there any doubt that the Sower of the seed is also the source of peace? "Peace I leave with you, My peace I give to you; not as the world gives" (John 14:27). When peace is absent, we're looking at the world, not at Him. "God is not the author of confusion but of peace" (1 Corinthians 14:33). He brings us the Gospel of peace (Romans 10:15) and preached peace far and near (Ephesians 2:17). How is this peace attained? "We have peace with God through our

Lord Jesus Christ" (Romans 5:1); it is multiplied through the knowledge of God (2 Peter 1:2) and yields the peaceable fruit of righteousness (Hebrews 12:11).

When we are obedient to Christ, He promises to guide our feet in the way of peace (Luke 1:79). "Great peace have those who love Your law, and nothing causes them to stumble" (Psalm 119:165). The Lord will also keep us in perfect peace when our minds are fixed on Him (Isaiah 26:3). He goes even further and says that He will speak peace to His people (Psalm 85:8), and will make even our enemies to be at peace with us (Proverbs 16:7).

As the Sower Himself has sown peace into our hearts, the Bible instructs us to sow peace along our paths, one believer to another (Romans 14:19), and to spread the Gospel of peace to those who are estranged from God (Romans 10:15). "Now the fruit of righteousness is sown in peace by those who make peace" (James 3:18).

Are you exercising the God-given fruit of sowing peace along your way?

Jesus
Is Longsuffering

The fruit of the Spirit is . . .
longsuffering {patience}.

(GALATIANS 5:22)

THE FRUIT THAT SPRINGS FORTH FROM THE GOOD SEED OF THE GOSPEL is imprinted with the spirit of patience. What comes to mind when you hear the word *patience*? Lost days of lingering? Dreadful delays? Passing the time? Waiting for an answer? The word *patience* actually speaks of strength, endurance, persistence, fortitude, staying power, vigor—a determined mind, a resilient will, a steadfast spirit, grit!

The patience of Job is an expression used even by the world. But many people may not realize that when they utter the phrase, they are actually quoting the Bible. Jesus' half brother James wrote, "Indeed we count them blessed who endure. You have heard of the *[patience] of Job* and seen the end intended by the Lord—that the Lord is very compassionate and merciful" (James 5:11). Job's legacy has stood the test of time, not because of his dreadful delay in hearing from God, or waiting on Him for an answer, or passing the time in the ash heap. Job's legacy lives on because of his grit. He exercised determination, resilience, and steadfastness in the midst of tragedy. How? Through patience—believing that God who was with him in good times would also be with him in bad times (Job 2:10).

This is the picture we see in the parable of the sower:

"But the [seed] that fell on the good ground are those who, having heard the word with a noble and good heart, keep it and bear fruit with patience" (Luke 8:15). While Job suffered every human heartache imaginable, he refused to curse God and die. Instead, he persevered. How can we possibly endure one tragedy after another without losing faith in God? The Bible says, "Whatever things were written before were written for our learning, that we through the patience and comfort of the Scriptures might have hope" (Romans 15:4). In the midst of deep suffering, Job said, "Though He slay me, yet will I trust Him" (Job 13:15). Job *patiently* hoped in God—he didn't let up. The Bible tells us that tribulation results in patience, experience, and hope (Romans 5:3–4). "No chastening seems to be joyful for the present, but painful; nevertheless, afterward it yields the peaceable fruit of righteousness to those who have been trained by it" (Hebrews 12:11).

First Timothy 6:11 tells us to run with patience, to pursue patience, and we're told to let patience have its perfect work (James 1:4). None of this is possible without "the God of patience" (Romans 15:5). The Sower implants the seed, and the Holy Spirit produces fruit when we grow in the knowledge of God. The seed is nourished and grows into fruit-bearing *patience.*

"Here is the patience of the saints; here are those who keep the commandments of God and the faith of Jesus" (Revelation 14:12). "Walk worthy of the Lord, fully pleasing Him, being fruitful in every good work . . . for all patience and longsuffering with joy" (Colossians 1:10–11).

Are you seeing the fruit of patience being produced in your life, even when things aren't going your way?

Jesus Is Kind

The fruit of the Spirit is . . . kindness.

(GALATIANS 5:22)

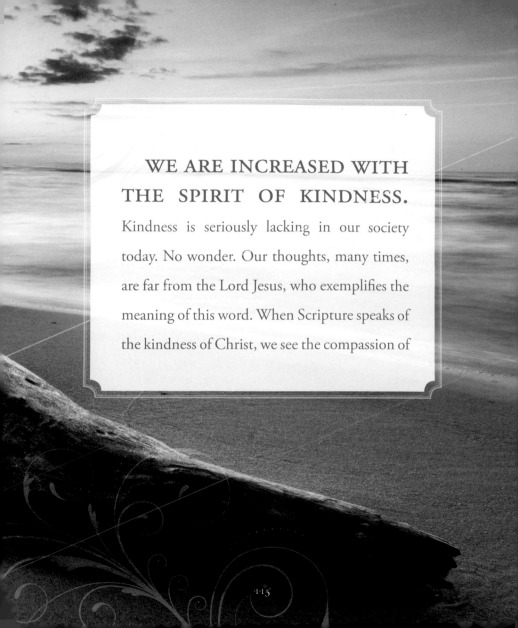

WE ARE INCREASED WITH THE SPIRIT OF KINDNESS.

Kindness is seriously lacking in our society today. No wonder. Our thoughts, many times, are far from the Lord Jesus, who exemplifies the meaning of this word. When Scripture speaks of the kindness of Christ, we see the compassion of

Christ. When He saw the multitudes bringing the sick, He had compassion and healed them (Matthew 14:14). When He saw the crowds with nothing to eat, He had compassion and fed them (Matthew 15:32); when He saw the crowd like sheep without a shepherd, He had compassion on them and began to teach them many things (Mark 6:34).

The fruit of kindness that the Lord exhibited is compelling. Jesus' kindness was so pure that Bible writers used many adjectives to convey this Christlike attribute. The Lord displayed His *marvelous* kindness (Psalm 31:21); His *merciful* kindness (Psalm 117:2); His *everlasting* kindness (Isaiah 54:8); His *great* kindness (Joel 2:13); and the *exceeding riches* . . . in His kindness (Ephesians 2:7). Every kind word He spoke, every kind act He did, every kind step He took paved the way to the cross, where the *most marvelous, great,* and *merciful* kindness toward mankind was offered to the lost world. "But when the kindness . . . of God our Savior toward man appeared. . . . He saved us" (Titus 3:4–5). The Lord is our example, and this is why we are told to "put on kindness" (Colossians 3:12).

When our heart produces the rotten fruit of harshness instead of graciousness, spitefulness instead of thoughtfulness, or maliciousness instead of gentleness, we are assisting Satan in his acts of cruelty against God's creation. The Bible says, "We are to God the fragrance of Christ among those who are being saved and among those who are perishing" (2 Corinthians 2:15). Are we living up to this marvelous standard?

Is your heart producing rotten fruit or the sweet-smelling savor of kindness?

The fruit of the Spirit is . . . goodness.

(GALATIANS 5:22)

WHEN THE GOSPEL SEED IS CULTIVATED IN THE FERTILE SOIL OF OUR SOUL, it illuminates our heart with the Spirit of goodness. The Bible says that no one is good; "No, not one" (Romans 3:10). So then, how are we to possess the fruit of goodness? The answer comes from the Spirit of God—it is His fruit of goodness, not ours. "The fruit of the Spirit is in all goodness, righteousness, and truth" (Ephesians 5:9). Lest we think ourselves good, Romans 3 tells us that we are all sinners and possess no good thing. Thankfully, the Bible later tells us, "Having been set free from sin . . . you have your fruit to holiness, and the end, everlasting life" (Romans 6:22). We were dead in sin but are now alive in Christ. The redeemed sinner is to *put on* Christ. We must speak His language, convey His heart, think His thoughts, walk in His footsteps, and wear His light. This is how we obey God's Word.

The redeemed are no longer seen by God as sinners. He sees those who are saved through His Son, Jesus Christ. That's why His Spirit can impart *goodness*. "Is the Spirit of the LORD restricted? Are these His doings? Do not My words do *good* to him who walks uprightly?" (Micah 2:7). "For God gives wisdom and knowledge and joy to a man who is good in His sight" (Ecclesiastes 2:26).

Jesus said, "I have called you friends, for all things that I heard from My Father I have made known to you . . . you should go and bear fruit" (John 15:15–16). Those of us who have received the Sower's seed will bear the fruit of the Spirit. Our moment-by-moment prayer should be, "Teach me to do Your will, for You are my God; Your Spirit is good" (Psalm 143:10). This is the only way we can possess *goodness*. When we receive Christ, He comes into our lives and we are partakers of His attributes. While many want to believe that God's riches mean gold and silver, His riches (the attributes of Himself) are far more bountiful and precious than man's idea of wealth (Proverbs 16:16). "The wisdom that is from above is first pure, then peaceable, gentle, willing to yield, full of mercy and *good* fruits" (James 3:17).

Willing to yield is an interesting phrase. When we are filled with God's Spirit, we have willingly surrendered what we possess—rotten fruit—for God's fruit, exchanging our evil for His *goodness.*

"And God is able to make all grace abound toward you, that you, always having all sufficiency in all things, may have an abundance for every *good* work" (2 Corinthians

9:8). "Walk worthy of the Lord, fully pleasing Him, being fruitful in every *good* work" (Colossians 1:10), and be "filled with the fruits of righteousness [goodness]" (Philippians 1:11). The psalmist declared, "Oh, taste and see that the LORD is good" (Psalm 34:8).

Will you pray daily that the Lord will infuse you with the fruit of goodness as you flourish in Him?

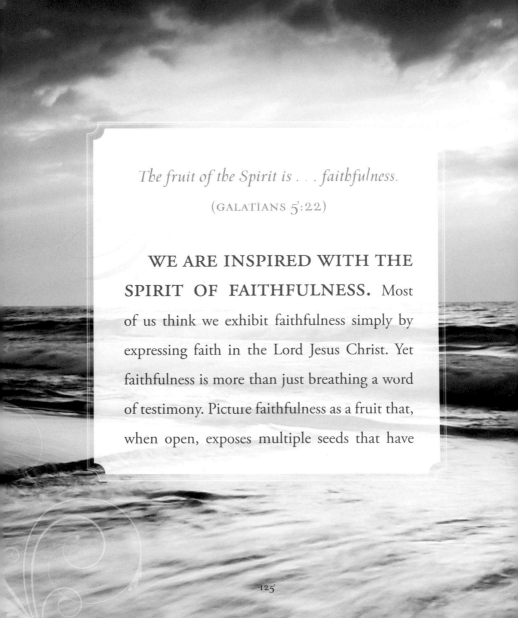

The fruit of the Spirit is . . . faithfulness.

(GALATIANS 5:22)

WE ARE INSPIRED WITH THE SPIRIT OF FAITHFULNESS. Most of us think we exhibit faithfulness simply by expressing faith in the Lord Jesus Christ. Yet faithfulness is more than just breathing a word of testimony. Picture faithfulness as a fruit that, when open, exposes multiple seeds that have the potential of reproducing more of the same fruit if sown, or planted, in rich soil.

These seeds inside the fruit of faithfulness can be described as reliable, trustworthy, dependable, dedicated, true, accurate—believable. This is a word picture of the Lord Jesus—the One who embodies all of these attributes. He imparts these to us when He sows the Gospel seed into our lives and forgives us for our sinful fruit of faith*less*ness. The Bible says, "If we confess our sins, He is faithful and just to forgive us our sins and to cleanse us from all unrighteousness" (1 John 1:9). It is because of His faithfulness that we can become men and women who are trustworthy servants of God, dependable spouses and children, dedicated worshipers, reliable employees, dependable employers, true friends, and believable witnesses.

The Lord Jesus increases our abilities by endowing us with His own virtues. "Grace and peace be multiplied to you . . . as His divine power has given to us all things that pertain to life and godliness . . . who called us by glory and virtue" (2 Peter 1:2–3). It is interesting to read these words from probably the roughest disciple of them all: the one who overreacted, spoke out of turn, and then turned around and did exactly what he said he would not do. Peter said he would be faithful to Jesus, and before he knew it, he denied the Lord and ran. Here we see a disciple who had grown from the milk of the Word, to the meat of the Word, and finally to the fruit of the Word. When Peter began to feed on the loveliness of the Lord Jesus, he grew strong in his faith and he became faithful. Jesus had sown a powerful seed in some shallow soil, but it took root. Then Peter passed on what the Lord passed on to him, telling others to add to their faith virtue, knowledge, self-control, perseverance, godliness, kindness, and love—the fruit of the Spirit. "For if these things are yours and abound," Peter writes, "you will be neither barren nor unfruitful" (2 Peter 1:8) as you live for Christ.

The Bible tells us that God is faithful (1 Corinthians 1:9) and the faithful Creator (1 Peter 4:19). He is faithful every night (Psalm 92:2); His counsel is faithful (Isaiah 25:1); His testimonies are faithful (Psalm 119:138); and His commandments are faithful (Psalm 119:86). We are told that Jesus Christ is the faithful witness (Revelation 1:5) and His name is Faithful and True (Revelation 19:11).

Because He has declared His faithfulness to man (Psalm 40:10), the Bible declares that man should also be found faithful (1 Corinthians 4:2). Jesus Christ promised to preserve the faithful, for He who calls you is faithful (1 Thessalonians 5:24). How does this happen? We become faithful as we hold fast to His faithful word (Titus 1:9) and speak His word faithfully (Jeremiah 23:28), for a faithful witness will not lie (Proverbs 14:5) but speak the truth—God's truth.

When the skin of your fruit is peeled back, will you be found faithful?

The fruit of the Spirit is . . . gentleness.

(GALATIANS 5:22–23)

AS THE GOSPEL SEED FLOURISHES IN OUR HEARTS, we are instilled with the Spirit of gentleness. "A servant of the Lord must . . . be gentle to all" (2 Timothy 2:24). This is what Paul wrote Timothy.

Paul told Titus to remind followers of Christ to be prepared for every good work, to speak evil of no man, and to be gentle, showing all humility to all men (Titus 3:1–2). Many times we overlook words in Scripture that seem insignificant. But here we see *all* mentioned twice: "showing *all* humility to *all* men." Naturally, no one ever comes in contact with "all" people, but this little word urges us to show complete humility toward everyone we come in contact with.

Timothy and Titus were Paul's spiritual sons, young men who had been saved under Paul's ministry. They bore fruit from the seed that Paul sowed while preaching the Word of God. These young pastors had their share of struggles, but Paul continued sowing truth into their lives, instructing, correcting, and encouraging them in the faith and in their leadership. Timothy and Titus encountered a great number of people from different backgrounds and persuasions. Paul emphasized the importance of being gentle, but then he described those who lack the gentle fruit of the Spirit and have no apparent interest in knowing Christ. "Avoid foolish disputes . . . contentions, and strivings about the law; for they are unprofitable and useless. Reject a divisive man after the first and second admonition, knowing that such a person is warped and sinning" (Titus 3:9–11).

You may feel that rejecting someone is not such a gentle approach, but nowhere in Scripture does the Lord instruct His followers to overlook, excuse, or accept another way other than God's way. This is why Jesus came: to show mankind "the way" (John 14:6). Subjecting ourselves to disputes, contentions, and strivings is not the way of following the gentle Savior. Paul pleaded with the Corinthians, warning them of false teachers in the church, but he pleaded with "the meekness and gentleness of Christ" (2 Corinthians 10:1). "Who is wise and understanding among you? Let him show by good conduct that his works are done in the meekness of wisdom . . . if you have . . . self-seeking in your hearts . . . this wisdom does not descend from above, but is earthly, sensual, demonic . . . but the wisdom that is from above is . . . gentle" (James 3:13–17).

Are you willing to show complete humility toward others as they observe the fruit of your gentle spirit?

The fruit of the Spirit is . . . self-control.
(GALATIANS 5:23)

THE SOWER'S SEED TAKING ROOT IN OUR HEART LEADS US

to be in step with the Spirit of self-control. The world has indulged itself with self-image, self-identity, self-esteem, and self-improvement. All of this creates a veneer of excessive self-promotion by gratifying every whim of appetite and desire.

If we are going to be indulgent, let's be extravagantly indulgent for the One who has

given us life and the will to live it for His glory. For Christians who seek after the things of Christ, they are not consumed with satisfying their flesh, which leads to corruption. The Bible tells us to sow to the Spirit and reap life everlasting (Galatians 6:8). We struggle with this in our mortal body, but God in His Word promises to help us when we are tempted and wrestling with the things of the world.

Jesus was an example to us in earthly form. Jesus "made Himself of no reputation, taking the form of a bondservant, and coming in the likeness of men. . . . He humbled Himself" (Philippians 2:7–8). Since He is the One we look to as the pattern for living, we are to "let nothing be done through selfish ambition or conceit . . . Let each of you look out not only for his own interests, but also for the interests of others (Philippians 2:3–4). Paul tells us to have no confidence in the flesh (Philippians 3:3).

Then he paints a word picture of the fruit of the Spirit that enables us to exercise restraint (self-control): Whatever things are true, noble, just, pure, lovely, of good report—if there is anything virtuous or worthy of praise—think on these things (Philippians 4:8).

Jesus is the source and example of self-control. When He cleanses our corrupt flesh and robes us in His righteousness, we become God-controlled—stepping out of self-indulgence into God-indulgence. We're not consumed with self-image because we know we are made in God's image (Genesis 1:26). We are not steeped in self-identification because we're identified with Christ: "That the life of Jesus also may be manifested in our body . . . that the life of Jesus also may be manifested in our mortal flesh . . . since we have the same spirit of faith" (2 Corinthians 4:10–11, 13). We don't have to clamor for self-esteem; instead, "in lowliness of mind let each esteem others better than himself" (Philippians 2:3). We don't have to constantly be running to self-improvement classes; we have been transformed by Christ (Romans 12:2). We don't have to undergo cosmetic alterations. Jesus Christ gives us a makeover the moment we step into His glorious forgiveness and newness of life. When He sends us out into the world, He has made us over by the fruit of His Spirit, with the command to go forth and sow seed that will produce an abundant harvest.

There is nothing more appetizing than to walk into a farmers' market and behold the appetizing, multicolored fruit overflowing in the baskets. Is this what our lives reflect? Does the world peer into our lives and see the gathering of bountiful fruit colored crimson that speaks of Christ's sacrificial love and the luscious yellow fruit as bright as God's eternal Light?

Has the Sower's seed in your life produced fruit so evident that it would cause others to taste and see that the Lord is good?

I am the true vine,
and My Father is the vinedresser.
Every branch in Me that does not bear fruit He takes away;
and every branch that bears fruit He prunes,
that it may bear more fruit.

(JOHN 15:1-2)

Lord, may the parable You spoke centuries ago
Spring forth with new life as Your Word
   is made known
May the seed of the Gospel find fertile ground
In the hearts of the lost the whole world 'round

If the seed is not buried in the soil of the heart
No life will take root and hope will depart
The winds of adversity will sweep it away
To the rocks and the briers and there it will lay

The birds will snatch seed and take to the air
Leaving the soul in the darkest despair
Some seed will settle in dry stony soil
Seared by the sun where roots cannot toil

May the seed not be carried by the doctrine of men
That lie among weeds where hearts do not bend
Or fall by the wayside where shallow it hides
Among the thorns and thistles that bind

May sowers handle the seed of Your Word
Planting it deep so Your Spirit is heard
Let the tears of many water through prayer
The seed of Your Gospel You've given to share

—DLT

Do you know the Sower of the seed? Rejoice in Him.

Has the seed been planted in the soil of your heart?
Receive from Him.

Are you a branch that is being nourished by the True
Vine? Remain in Him.

WORTHY

IF YOU LIKED THIS BOOK . . .

- Tell your friends by going to: www.thesower.net and clicking "LIKE"

- Log on to facebook.com/worthypublishing page, click "LIKE" and post a comment regarding what you enjoyed about the book

- Tweet "I recommend reading #TheSowerBook by Franklin Graham & Donna Lee Toney @Worthypub"

- Hashtag: #TheSower

- Subscribe to our newsletter by going to www.worthypublishing.com

Worthy Publishing
Facebook Page

Worthy Publishing
Website